First World War
and Army of Occupation
War Diary
France, Belgium and Germany

21 DIVISION
Divisional Troops
Divisional Cyclist Company
9 September 1915 - 30 April 1916

WO95/2141/2

The Naval & Military Press Ltd
www.nmarchive.com
Published in association with The National Archives

Published by

The Naval & Military Press Ltd

Unit 10 Ridgewood Industrial Park,

Uckfield, East Sussex,

TN22 5QE England

Tel: +44 (0) 1825 749494

www.naval-military-press.com

www.nmarchive.com

This diary has been reprinted in facsimile from the original. Any imperfections are inevitably reproduced and the quality may fall short of modern type and cartographic standards.

© **Crown Copyright**
Images reproduced by permission of The National Archives, London, England, 2015.

Contents

Document type	Place/Title	Date From	Date To
Heading	WO95/2141/2 Divisional Cyclist Company 1915-Sept 1916 Jan		
Heading	21st Division 21st Divl Cyclist Coy Sep 1915-Jan 1916		
Heading	21st Division 21st Divl. Cycl. Coy Vol I Sept 15		
War Diary	?ands Wittey Camp	09/09/1915	09/09/1915
War Diary	Southampton	09/09/1915	09/09/1915
War Diary	Le Havre	10/09/1915	10/09/1915
War Diary	St Omer	11/09/1915	11/09/1915
War Diary	Watten	12/09/1915	21/09/1915
War Diary	Omer	22/09/1915	22/09/1915
War Diary	Ferfay	23/09/1915	24/09/1915
War Diary	Hallicourt	25/09/1915	25/09/1915
War Diary	Les District	26/09/1915	27/09/1915
War Diary	North Of Vermelles	28/09/1915	28/09/1915
War Diary	Bethune	29/09/1915	29/09/1915
War Diary	Ami	30/09/1915	30/09/1915
War Diary	Liettres	30/09/1915	30/09/1915
Heading	21st Division 21st Div. Cyclist Coy Vol 2 Oct 15		
War Diary	Blessy	01/10/1915	01/10/1915
War Diary	Morbecque	02/10/1915	02/10/1915
War Diary	Strazeele	03/10/1915	31/10/1915
Heading	27th Div Cyclist Coy Vol 3 Nov 15		
War Diary	Strazeele	01/11/1915	12/11/1915
War Diary	Armentieres	13/11/1915	30/11/1915
Heading	21st Cyclist 4 Vol 5		
War Diary	Armentieres	01/12/1915	01/01/1916
Heading	21st Divisional Troops 21st Divisional Cyclist Company January 1916 Attached Report On Raid 25/26th		
War Diary	Armentieres	01/01/1916	31/01/1916
Heading	Report On Raid 25th 26th January 1916		
War Diary	Armentieres	25/01/1916	26/01/1916
Heading	21st Divisional Troops 21st Divisional Cyclist Company February 1916		
War Diary	Armentieres	01/02/1916	29/02/1916
Heading	21st Divisional Troops 21st Divisional Cyclist Company March 1916		
Heading	21 Div Cyclist Vol 7		
War Diary	Armentieres	01/03/1916	21/03/1916
War Diary	Merris	21/03/1916	30/03/1916
War Diary	Ribemont	31/03/1916	31/03/1916
Heading	21st Divisional Troops Became XV Corps Cyclists 10.3.16 21st Divisional Cyclist Company April 1916		
War Diary	Ribemont	01/04/1916	30/04/1916

WO 95/2141/2

DIVISION Cyclist Compy

1915 - Sept   1916 JAN

21ST DIVISION

21ST DIVL CYCLIST COY.

SEP 1915 - JAN 1916

21st Kinnaird

12/7083

20th Sikh: Geh: Coy
Vol I

Sep! 15

In reserve behind Lens
21/9/15

September 1915

Army Form C. 2118.

WAR DIARY
or
INTELLIGENCE SUMMARY.
(Erase heading not required.)

21st Divisional Cyclist Company

Instructions regarding War Diaries and Intelligence Summaries are contained in F.S. Regs., Part II. and the Staff Manual respectively. Title pages will be prepared in manuscript.

Hour, Date, Place	Summary of Events and Information	Remarks and references to Appendices
4:30 AM 9/9/15. Uplands Witley Camp.	Left for Southampton	
7am Southampton	Embarked on ship and sailed for France 7.30pm	
10 9/9/15 9am Le Havre 10.30am	Disembarked Left in train	Weather very fine
11 9/9/15 4.30am St Omer	Arrived and marched to Watten	
12 9/9/15 Watten	Billeted 12ᵗʰ – 20ᵗʰ	
19 9/9/15 "	Football Match v A.S.C. Won 6-0	
20 9/9/15 " 5.30pm	Left for Watten arrived 12 M.N.	
21 9/9/15 Watten 7pm	Left for Amiens arrived 10pm	
22 9/9/15 Amiens 7pm	Left for Fayay arrived 8.30pm	
23 9/9/15 Fayay	Football Match v S. Irish Horse Lost 4-2	
24 9/9/15 Fayay 6pm	Left for Vallecourt. Arrived 3 and N.E. of Vallecourt 10pm	Rain night 24/25

September 1915

Army Form C. 2118.

WAR DIARY
or
INTELLIGENCE SUMMARY. 21st Divisional Cyclist Coy

(Erase heading not required.)

Hour, Date, Place	Summary of Events and Information	Remarks and references to Appendices
2 p.m. 25/9/15 Hallicourt	Left and marched to West of Vermelles	Rainy Weather
6 a.m. 26/9/15 Loos district	Attack by the British Troops commenced 21st Div. got into action. Div. killed Troops	"
4 p.m. " "	in reserve. 8 officers Total reconnoitre battle field 5.30 p.m – 6 p.m	
10.30 a.m – 4.30 p.m 27/9/15	Company collected wounded. Casualties in Company 4 killed, 2 wounded, 2 missing	Fine
28/9/15 North of Vermelles	Bivouaced in Div. Reserve	
8 p.m " " Bethune	Marched to Bethune. Billeted in Schools myself & staff	
3 p.m 29/9/15	Left for Arc. Arrived there Billeted in Barracks night 29/7/31 to	Rainy Weather
10 a.m 30/9/15 Arc	Left on reclain arrived 2 p.m	
" " Lattre	29/9/11 to Bloay Arrived 6 p.m. Billeted night 30 Sept / 1 October	

R H Morgan
2nd Lieut Coy
Cmdg. 21st Cyclist Coy.

121/7517

21st Hussars.

21st Bn L. Gelot Coy
Vol 2
Oct. 15

Army Form C. 2118.

WAR DIARY
of
INTELLIGENCE SUMMARY.
21st Div. Cyclist Coy

OCTOBER 1915

(Erase heading not required.)

Instructions regarding War Diaries and Intelligence Summaries are contained in F. S. Regs., Part II. and the Staff Manual respectively. Title pages will be prepared in manuscript.

Hour, Date, Place 1915	Summary of Events and Information	Remarks and references to Appendices
6.30 AM 1st October 1915 BLESSY.	Left and marched to MORBECQUE. Arrived 9.30 AM. Billeted night 1/2 Oct.	H.m.B.
8.30 AM 2nd " MORBECQUE.	Left and " STRAZEELE " 9.30 AM. Billeted	H.m.B.
3rd " STRAZEELE.	Church Parade 10.30 AM. Football Match v S. Staff. Area 3pm. Won 3-0	H.m.B.
4th " "	Officers reconnoitre Billeting Area N.W. of HAZEBROUCK	H.m.B.
5th " "	Officers conducting billeting parties of Div Artillery & also numerous area	H.m.B.
6th " "	Officers reconnoitring Billeting Area E. of HAZEBROUCK	H.m.B.
7th " "	Camp Routine and Training	H.m.B.
8th " "	Officers reconnoitring Billeting Area N.E. of HAZEBROUCK	H.m.B.
9th " "	Camp Routine and Training	H.m.B.
10th " "	Church Parade 11 AM. Inspection by G.O.C. Div 4.30 pm.	H.m.B.
11th " "	Camp Routine and Training	H.m.B.
12th " "	" " "	H.m.B.
13th " "	Holy Communion Service 6.30 AM. Tactical Training Scheme 9.30 AM – 2.30 pm.	H.m.B.
14th " "	Camp Routine and Training	H.m.B.
15th " "	" " "	H.m.B.
16th " "	" " "	H.m.B.
17th " "	Church Parade at Div H.Q. 9 AM.	H.m.B.
18th " "	Officers reconnoitring Railways (HAZEBROUCK – BAILLEUL) (HAZEBROUCK – POPERINGHE)	H.m.B.

Army Form C. 2118.

WAR DIARY
INTELLIGENCE SUMMARY.
(Erase heading not required.)

21st Div Cyclist Coy.

OCTOBER 1915.

Instructions regarding War Diaries and Intelligence Summaries are contained in F.S. Regs., Part II. and the Staff Manual respectively. Title pages will be prepared in manuscript.

Hour, Date, Place 1915	Summary of Events and Information	Remarks and references to Appendices
19th October STRAZEELE.	Officer reconnoitering Billeting Area S.E. of BAILLEUL	A.M.B.
20th "	Water inspection by Officer in area N. of STRAZEELE.	A.M.B.
21 "	Officers reconnoitering roads in Div: Area.	A.M.B.
22 "	Camp Routine and training	A.M.B.
23rd "	" "	A.M.B.
24th "	Church Parade at Div: H.Q. 9 A.M.	A.M.B.
25th "	Camp Routine and training	A.M.B.
26th "	" "	A.M.B.
27th "	2nd Corps Inspection by His Majesty the King, at BAILLEUL 2:30 P.M.	A.M.B.
28th "	This Company represented by 1 Officer and 20 men.	A.M.B.
"	Camp Routine and training	A.M.B.
29th "	" "	A.M.B.
30th "	" "	A.M.B.
31st "	Church Parade at Div: H.Q. 10 A.M.	A.M.B.
	During the month Officers, N.C.O's have attended lectures and classes at the Corps and Div: Schools for instruction in Grenadier Work.	

27th Bgi: Cycl: Coy:
Vol. 3

121/7656

Nov 15

Army Form C. 2118.

WAR DIARY
or
INTELLIGENCE SUMMARY.
(Erase heading not required.)

21st Div: Cyclist Coy.

Hour, Date, Place	Summary of Events and Information	Remarks and references to Appendices
November 1. STRAZEELE.	Training in Grenadier Work and use of Shering Gun.	H.m.R.
" 2 "	"	H.m.R.
" 3 "	"	H.m.R.
" 4 "	"	H.m.R.
" 5 "	"	H.m.R.
" 6 "	Company Parade and Camp Routine. Church Parade 10 a.m.	H.m.R.
" 7 "		H.m.R.
" 8 "	Training in Grenadier Work and use of Shering Gun.	H.m.R.
" 9 "	"	H.m.R.
" 10 "	"	H.m.R.
" 11 "	Preparing to move.	H.m.R.
" 12 "	Left STRAZEELE for ARMENTIERES. 9 A.M. Arrived at Armentieres 12 noon. Took over Bridge Guards and Ammunition from 50th Div Cyclist Coy. One Platoon detailed to assist A.P.M. until relieved. On men remanded to Div: H.R. Guard.	H.m.R.

Army Form C. 2118.

WAR DIARY
or
INTELLIGENCE SUMMARY. 21st Div. Cyclist Coy.
(Erase heading not required.)

Instructions regarding War Diaries and Intelligence Summaries are contained in F.S. Regs., Part II. and the Staff Manual respectively. Title pages will be prepared in manuscript.

Hour, Date, Place	Summary of Events and Information	Remarks and references to Appendices
November 13 ARMENTIERES	The Company reorganised into 5 Platoons. Rifle Grenade Platoon, Grenade Platoon, Stokes Gun Platoon and two Cyclist Platoons.	Hd.Qrs.
" 14 "	Church Parade at Div: H.Q. 6(nine) officers, eleven officers reconnoitre Divisional front.	Hd.Qrs.
" 15 "	Officers continue reconnaissance of Div. front.	Hd.Qrs.
" 16 "	2 Squads + 1 Corpnis fart of the R.G. Platoon fired 5mm. in trenches in trench No. 74. 7.30 a.m. 12 Sighting shots 8.30 a.m. The officer of the R.G. Platoon slightly wounded in head at 9.30 a.m. 4 Grenades then fired into enemies Trenches. Replied to by enemies artillery.	Hd.Qrs.
" 17 "	The R.G. Platoon in trenches as on the previous day. 70 firing of Grenades. Shelled by enemy.	Hd.Qrs.
" 18 "	8.30 a.m. — 9.40 a.m. R.G. Platoon fired 160 rounds of enemy with success. 100 rounds landing in enemies Trench. Damage also caused to enemies wire entanglements. Armentieres shelled. Murdered & cellars. 16 casualties.	Hd.Qrs.

Forms/C. 2118/10   (9.29.6) W 4141—463 100,000 9/14 H W V

Army Form C. 2118.

WAR DIARY
or
INTELLIGENCE SUMMARY.
(Erase heading not required.)

A.J. Div: Cyclist Coy.

Instructions regarding War Diaries and Intelligence Summaries are contained in F.S. Regs., Part II. and the Staff Manual respectively. Title pages will be prepared in manuscript.

Hour, Date, Place	Summary of Events and Information	Remarks and references to Appendices
November 19. ARMENTIERES.	Training in Grenadework & use of Stores & Guns	Nov B.
" 20. "	"	Nov B.
" 21. "	Church Parade at Div: H.Q. 9 a.m.	Nov B.
" 22. "	2 Squads of R.G. Platoon. One working in Trench 89 and the other in Trench 88 opened fire at 4'45 p.m. and continued with intervals until 9.30 p.m. Party in Trench 88 obtained 30 & 90 Direct hits into enemies Trench. Party in Trench 89 Lado Farm. The enemy replied with 10 Rifle Grenades and 12 Trench Mortar Shells. Casualties. One man Killed.	Nov B.
" 23. "	Training in Grenadier Work & use of Spraying Gun	Nov B.
" 24. "	"	Nov B.
" 25. "	"	Nov B.
" 26. "	"	Nov B.
" 27. "	"	Nov B.
" 28. "	"	Nov B.
" 29. "	Church Parade at Div: H.Q. 9 a.m.	Nov B.
" 30. "	Instruction 1 Div: Grenade Stn.	Nov B.

2.° Geb.
1 Vol. #5

12
7911

Vol 4.

WAR DIARY or **INTELLIGENCE SUMMARY.**

Army Form C. 2118.

Place: Ploegsteert Wood, Belgium Sheet 36 40000

Army Corps: 21st Divisional Cyclist Coy.

Month: DECEMBER

(Erase heading not required.)

Hour, Date, Place		Summary of Events and Information	Remarks and references to Appendices
December	1st ARMENTIERES	Construction of Div. Grenade Store	Lyn B.
"	2nd "	Construction of Div. Grenade Store	4 R.B.
"	3rd "	Construction of Div. Grenade Store	H.W.B.
"	4th "	Two Sections of Rifle Grenade Platoon in Trenches in Trench 80 (C.29c) at 11 p.m. fired 140 rounds at 6 in. with excellent result. In accordance with instructions to followed at 6.15 p.m. our Artillery fired enemies parked wire in afternoon. The Catapult Platoon (North) sent Spans and Goliath operated with the R.G. Platoon and did good work.	H.W.B.
"	5th "	Stokes Brass at Bois VR. 9 p.m. Construction of Div. Grenade Store.	H.W.B.
"	6th "	Construction of Div. Grenade Store.	H.W.B.
"	7th "	3 Sections of R.G. Platoon fired Grenades in Enemies Trenches in Trench 70 (I.14c) 12 noon - 1 p.m. 180 Grenades fired causing considerable damage to enemies	
"	8th "	Spring Gun of the S.G. Platoon fired from Trench 74 (I.5c). Firing 5.3 rounds in the front aspect.	H.W.B.

Forms/C. 2118/10

(9 29 6) W 4141—463 100,000 9/14 H W V

Army Form C. 2118.

WAR DIARY
or
INTELLIGENCE SUMMARY.
(Erase heading not required.)

of 1st Div. Cy Chief Eng.

Instructions regarding War Diaries and Intelligence Summaries are contained in F.S. Regs., Part II. and the Staff Manual respectively. Title pages will be prepared in manuscript.

Hour, Date, Place		Summary of Events and Information	Remarks and references to Appendices
December	ARMENTIERES		
9 a		Superintending of Div. Grenade Stores	Apx B.
10 a	"	Superintending of Div. Grenade Stores	Apx B.
11 a	"	Drill Parade & Kit Inspection	Apx B.
12 a	"	Church Parade at Div. H.Q. 9 am.	Apx B.
13 M	"	Rev. & March. 2 Officers Grenade Officers + N.C.Os from 2nd Div.	Apx B.
		(Mounted Section) arrived instructing cm.	
		Construction of Div. Grenade Store	Apx B.
		Div. Artillery fired trench mortars, bursts more in front	
		of trenches 69, 70 & 71 preparatory to a "cutting out"	
		(I.N.C. & I.S.E.)	
14 A	"	expedition by 120 Officers & men of 1st & 8th Lancashire	
15 A	"	Light Infantry. Germans being much alarmed, opened up	Apx B.
		unu billets & the expedition lasting 15 minutes	
Night 15/16		commencing at 3.10 am. The R.F. Staten of the by	
		supplied covering fire on both flanks & experience	
		front gun smoke heavy shell plus not good	
		effect. No casualties.	
16		Construction of Div. Grenade Store.	Apx B.

WAR DIARY
or
INTELLIGENCE SUMMARY.
(Erase heading not required.)

Army Form C. 2118.

of 1st Div: G. Staff Coy.

Hour, Date, Place	Summary of Events and Information	Remarks and references to Appendices
December 17 ARMENTIERES	Construction of Div: Grenade Store.	Hon: B.
" 18 "	Instruction of Div: Grenade Store.	Hon: B.
" 19 "	Church Parade 9 a.m. R.E. Platoon attached to Ptroles. (I 16.10.) — Started by 2 N.C.M. but were not used. Returned 3 p.m.	Hon: B.
" 20 "	Construction of Div: Grenade Store.	Hon: B.
" 21 "	R.E. Platoon, S.G. Platoon, & Batifields Platoon (S.I.H)	Hon: B.
Night 21/22	2 Squads front came in trenches in the "MUSHROOM". reached 70 (Time) at 6 p.m. Two squads joined intermittently throughout the night & were onlay turning in no case in front of the trenches.	Hon: B.
22/23	A 6 Squads arrived at entrance trenches night. Killed by enemy. Casualties: Soner killed (S.I.H.)	Hon: B.
Night 23/24	The 6 squads worked on trenches night.	Hon: B.
" 25 "	Christmas Day. Church Parade 9.15 a.m. Sky C	Hon: B.
" 26 "	Construction of intheorith Church Parade at D.H.Q. 9.15 a.m.	Hon: B.

WAR DIARY
or
INTELLIGENCE SUMMARY.
(Erase heading not required.)

Army Form C. 2118.

2nd Div. Cyclist Coy.

Hour, Date, Place	Summary of Events and Information	Remarks and references to Appendices
December 27. ARMENTIERES	R.G. Platoon, S.G. Platoon, and Cab. Tpt. Platoon one Sgnal. from each in position in Armentieres at 11.15 a.m. Artillery bombardment Pérones started 12.45 p.m. The above signals joined with enemies Circles, other bombardment and good results. The enemy replied with a long bombardment. Casualties 2 W. & 1 Kd. (Cyclist: One L.M.G. (Lt. Hughes.))	Am. B.
" Mgr F.137/48	One Sgnal of R Grenadiers in Armentieres	Am. B.
" 28/29	One Sgnal of R Grenadiers in Armentieres	Am. B.
" 29/30	One Sgnal of R Grenadiers in Armentieres	Am. B.
" 30/31	One Sgnal of R Grenadiers in Armentieres	Am. B.
" 31/1/16	One Sgnal of R Grenadiers in Armentieres	Am. B.

O.McKay Major
Cmndg. 2nd Div. Cyclist Coy.

21st Divisional Troops

21st DIVISIONAL CYCLIST COMPANY ::: JANUARY 1916

Attached:- Report oh RAID 25/26th.

WAR DIARY
or
INTELLIGENCE SUMMARY.
(Erase heading not required.)

Army Form C. 2118.

Instructions regarding War Diaries and Intelligence Summaries are contained in F.S. Regs., Part II. and the Staff Manual respectively. Title pages will be prepared in manuscript.

Hour, Date, Place	Summary of Events and Information	Remarks and references to Appendices
Armentières Jan 1st 1916.	One squad of Rifle Grenadiers in the Mushroom for the night.	1st Div Cyclists
" 2.	" " " " " " " " "	
" 3.	" " " " " " " " "	
" 4.	Drill parades.	
" 5.	" "	
" 6.	At 2 am. 1 officer + 20 men sent for a spy who has recently been shooting at sentries. ett night a party of 5 officers + 90 men picketed the ARMENTIÈRES - HOUPLINES Rly. from 5.30pm to 7am. on the 7th to catch the same spy. No success.	
" 7.	1 officer + 20 men stand fast at night in case of need to continue spy hunt.	
" 8.	Parade to clean billet etc.	
" 9.	ett 12.30 a.m. 3 officers + 30 men again hunt for spy. No success. Church parade at 9 AM.	
" 10.	Grenadier training.	
" 11.	Rifle Grenadier platoon, 1 squad West Spring gun, + catapult platoon S.I.H. engaged in a bombardment from 12 am - 1pm. 2 squads R.E. in 70. 1 " R.G. + catapults in 75. 1 " R.G. + Spring gun in 88.	

Army Form C. 2118.

WAR DIARY
or
INTELLIGENCE SUMMARY.
(Erase heading not required.)

21st Div Cyclists

Hour, Date, Place	Summary of Events and Information	Remarks and references to Appendices
Armentières Jan 11th 1916	(continued) Shooting remarkably good. 4 casualties in trench 75 - 1 killed & 2 wounded by premature burst of a Newton Rifle Grenade, the former S.I.H. the 2 latter eyelets, +1 S.I.H. wounded by shrapnel.	
" 12th 1916.	Grenade training Gas helmet drill	
" 13th "	" "	
" 14th "	Bathing parade etc.	
" 15th "	Grenade training	
" 16th "	Church parade in morning. Live grenade throwing in the afternoon.	
" 17th "	Grenade training + bayonet fighting.	
" 18th "	" "	
" 19th "	Party sent up to Mushroom (40 rank) for instruction. Another party sent up to Mushroom for instruction	
" 20th "	Grenade + bayonet practice	
" 21st "	" "	
" 22nd "	" "	
" 23rd "	Church parade in morning. Afternoon + evening practice attacks on trenches at grenade school.	

Army Form C. 2118.

WAR DIARY
or
INTELLIGENCE SUMMARY.
(Erase heading not required.)

2nd Devon Regiment

Hour, Date, Place	Summary of Events and Information	Remarks and references to Appendices
Armentières. Jan 24th 1916.	Practice attacks on trenches at Grenade school.	
" 25th "	Inspection by G.O.C. Div. at 8 A.M. Party of 50 men + 4 officers delivered an attack on the German trenches opposite the Mushroom, but the enemy was on the alert, + a bombing patrol discovered us before we were in position. After a temporary check the advance was continued but the enemy sent up Very lights when we had nearly reached his wire, + opened rapid fire on us. As a surprise was impossible the party retired under heavy fire losing 2 officers + 6 men killed + 3 wounded. Another man was wounded while retiring.	
" 26th "	Rifle grenade in the front trench.	
" 27th "	Cleaning billets, clothes + equipment. Kit inspection. Bathing parade.	
" 28th "	Relieved the infantry who had taken over some of our guards. Funeral of 2Lt. Hall + Pte. Woodcock, killed on 25th. Party sent up to fetch Rifle stands not in 25th. One man killed by shot from a fixed rifle.	

Army Form C. 2118.

WAR DIARY
or
INTELLIGENCE SUMMARY.
(Erase heading not required.)

Instructions regarding War Diaries and Intelligence Summaries are contained in F.S. Regs., Part II. and the Staff Manual respectively. Title pages will be prepared in manuscript.

Hour, Date, Place	Summary of Events and Information	Remarks and references to Appendices
Armentières Jan 29th 1916.	Cleaning billet & drill parades.	
" " 30th. "	Church parade at 9.15 a.m. Funeral of Lt. Smith & The. Beaver at 2.30 p.m.	
" " 31. "	Practice in crossing knife-rests with roller mats & in bridging sunken wire, followed by trench clearing at Trench Warfare School.	

REPORT ON RAID 25th/26th January 1916

WAR DIARY or INTELLIGENCE SUMMARY

Army Form C. 2118.

21st Divisional Cyclist Co

Place	Date	Hour	Summary of Events and Information	Remarks and references to Appendices
Armentières	Jan 25/26		Having got permission from the G.O.C. a party of 5 officers and about 50 other ranks under the command of Major Kay made a raid on the enemy's trenches opposite "The Mushroom" a point about 60 yards from the German lines. The party was divided into 3 Bombing Squads each consisting of 1 officer + 8 other ranks, 2 Bayonet Squads under 1 officer, also Rifle & hat men (for carrying one) wire cutters + scouts. After the attack had been launched it was discovered that either by accident a previous warning the Germans were expecting us. Very lights suddenly went up + were met by bombs from a crater on our left, + Rifle fire from Germans lying on the parapet + also in the front line which had been made the previous day by our artillery. The Germans were firing on us from a distance of about 30 + 40 yards from the outside of the party and their numbers been about 70 if them opposing us. After replying to their fire + carrying then a front many casualties with bombs + rifle fire a retirement was ordered + carried out very steadily under a very heavy fire.	Supplementing to entry in Diary of January 1916.

2/

2nd Div. Gibraltar

Army Form C. 2118.

WAR DIARY

INTELLIGENCE SUMMARY.
(Erase heading not required.)

Place	Date	Hour	Summary of Events and Information	Remarks and references to Appendices
			The Casualties were 2 Officers & 6 men killed & 3 wounded. The top used in the preliminary advance & portion of assembly outside in wire, owing to its narrowness proved an obstacle both in the advance & retreat. In process of recognition & the less conspicuous the party had their fires and hands blacked & wore fine helmets rolled up (which proved too light). The premature abandonment of the advanced turning posts by the infantry holding the trenches, thus allowing the Germans time to crater materially affected the success of the operation.	Supplementary to entry in Diary of January

R.J Kay Major
Camdy. 2nd Div Cyclist Coy.

21st Divisional Troops

21st DIVISIONAL CYCLIST COMPANY ::: FEBRUARY 1916

Army Form C. 2118.

WAR DIARY
or
INTELLIGENCE SUMMARY.
(Erase heading not required.)

Cyclist Company
21st Division

Instructions regarding War Diaries and Intelligence Summaries are contained in F.S. Regs., Part II. and the Staff Manual respectively. Title pages will be prepared in manuscript.

Place	Date	Hour	Summary of Events and Information	Remarks and references to Appendices
Armentières	February 1st	10 am	Demonstration of crossing of high, low, sunken barbed wire by a party of 2 officers + 26 men at the French Warfare School. Roller-mats, wooden-bridges were used + the Corps + Army Commanders expressed themselves as quite totally pleased with the work. The Army Commander complimented us on the attack of the 25th January.	
	2nd		Gas helmet drill. Instruction in bombing + drill parades.	
	3rd		Practice at grenade school for demonstration on next day. Drill parades.	
	4th		Demonstration at Div. Grenade School for senior officers of the use of Rifle Grenades, Spring guns, + catapults.	
	5th		Cleaning billet etc.	
	6th	9.15 am	Church parade.	
	7th		Instruction in bombing of new draft of 16 men. Remainder route-march + Drill.	
	8th		Bombing instruction.	
	9th		" "	
	10th		" " + bathing parade. Consequent on report sent in to Corps H.Q. following was received from Army H.Q. "Ref. G.941 (6524) dated 4/2/16 the Army Commander has read of the work	

WAR DIARY
or
INTELLIGENCE SUMMARY.
(Erase heading not required.)

Army Form C. 2118.

Cyclist Company
21st Division

Place	Date	Hour	Summary of Events and Information	Remarks and references to Appendices
Armentières	February 10th		done by the 21st Div. Cyclist Coy on the night of the 25/26th January with great interest. "The spirit which led this Cyclist Coy to undertake the operation is worthy of the highest praise. He regrets the losses that occurred. He wishes you to convey to all concerned his appreciation of their gallant conduct under very trying circumstances." "He is very glad to have had an opportunity of inspecting the unit on parade & hopes that in its next effort it will attain the success which it has shown it thoroughly deserves.	
	11th		Demonstration at Div. Grenade School for senior officers on same lines as last week. Position selected in 79/80 trenches for combined bombardment by mechanical throwers of Pont Ballot salient.	
	12th		Two officers with parties to work Trifle stands, & A Spring guns with a catapult party of S.I.H. in 79/80 trench for bombardment of German trenches, at dusk (5.15pm) by smoke bombs to make enemy expect an attack man their trenches. Very effective shooting by S. Guns. The bombs had the desired effect of leading enemy to expect an attack + gas signals red rockets for reinforcements were noticed immediately air opened fire.	

Army Form C. 2118.

WAR DIARY
or
INTELLIGENCE SUMMARY.
(Erase heading not required.)

Cyclist Coy.
21st Division.

Place	Date	Hour	Summary of Events and Information	Remarks and references to Appendices
Armentières	February 12th		The Rifle Grenadiers did good shooting on the flanks of the salient. The RA then bombarded the enemy's front line & supports for 20 minutes — to 5:40 pm with good effect. Operations ceased at 5:45. Heavy retaliation but no casualties amongst our men.	
	13th	9.15am	Church Parade at D.H.Q.	
	14th		Instruction in grenade work & drill parades. Party sent up to bring down the guns.	
	15th		Drill parade. Two new officers taken on the strength.	
	16th		Gas helmet drill & bombing instruction.	
	17th		Bathing parade & drill. Coy. Kit inspection.	
	18th		" " Trench work at grenade school.	
	19th		Cleaning billet	
	20th	9.15am	Church parade. Bombing instruction at school in the p.m.	
	21st		Route-march & cycle cleaning	
	22nd		Physical drill & drill parade.	
	23rd		Kit inspection. Party take up 2 spring-guns & 2 catapults (S.I.H.) to dump for Y3 trench	
	24th		Guns billed in the morning; & at 11pm fired smoke bombs into the Ply. salient opposite trench 1943.	

Army Form C. 2118.

WAR DIARY
or
INTELLIGENCE SUMMARY.
(Erase heading not required.)

Cyclist Coy
21st Division

Place	Date	Hour	Summary of Events and Information	Remarks and references to Appendices
Armentières	February 24th		Wind being E.N.E. rather neutralised the effect by blowing some of the smoke back towards our trenches (Y1) on the right. Enemy's retaliation slight. No casualties.	
	25th	11 am	Party of officers, NCOs, men, of Cyclists & 31H (attached) attend demonstration of Flammenwerfer at Div. Grenade School.	
	27th	9.15 am	Church parade & C. to Professionals. Owing to rain x-new trench practice at Grenade School postponed.	
	28th		Route march. Trench work of bombing squad at trench warfare school.	
	29th		Drill parade. Bomb throwing at F.W. School	

A/MayMayor
A/Lt Cyclists

Comdg. 21st Div Cyclists

21st Divisonal Troops

21st DIVISIONAL CYCLIST COMPANY ::: MARCH 1916

Ref. No. H.A. 127.

Secret.

To:-
 D.A.G.,
  Base.

21 D.W Cyclists Co Vol 7

Herewith War Diary for the month of March, 1916.

8.4/16.

W.H. Ritter. Lieut. for Major,
Commanding, 21st Div. Cyclists

Army Form C. 2118.

WAR DIARY
or
INTELLIGENCE SUMMARY.
(Erase heading not required.)

Instructions regarding War Diaries and Intelligence Summaries are contained in F. S. Regs., Part II. and the Staff Manual respectively. Title pages will be prepared in manuscript.

Place	Date 1916.	Hour	Summary of Events and Information	Remarks and references to Appendices
Armentières	March 1		Drill parade + kit inspection. Cricket Match versus S.F.A. during the afternoon.	
"	2		Drill + bathing parade.	
"	3		Drill + bathing parade.	
"	4		Cleaning billet. Grenade training continued but outdoor work hindered by continued falls of snow. Sudden shelling by enemy at 5 p.m. New salvo into cellars, but bombardment ceased quickly. No casualties in the company.	
"	5		Church parade at 9.15 a.m.	
"	6		Intelligence squad (12 men + 1 officer) of No. 2 platoon commence Divisional Intelligence Work: investigating shelled areas.	
"	7		Company parade as usual for physical drill.	
"	8		Company parade as usual for physical drill + distributing of cycles. Further work by Intelligence squad during p.m.	
"	9		Drill + bathing parade. Foot inspection.	
"	10		Bathing parade. Instruction in Map Reading. Company P.o.d.	

T2134. Wt. W708—776. 500000. 4/15. Sir J. C. & S.

Army Form C. 2118.

Instructions regarding War Diaries and Intelligence
Summaries are contained in F. S. Regs., Part II.
and the Staff Manual respectively. Title pages
will be prepared in manuscript.

WAR DIARY
or
INTELLIGENCE SUMMARY.
(Erase heading not required.)

Place	Date 1916	Hour	Summary of Events and Information	Remarks and references to Appendices
Armentières	March 11		Tour of trenches by parties of 3 officers + 6 men, round each sector to familiarise them with the approaches to different trenches.	
"	12		Church Parade at 9.15 a.m.	
"	13		Physical + steadying drill. Bombing practice at Trench Warfare School.	
"	14		Bombing practice + kit inspection.	
"	15		Map Reading.	
"	16		Bathing Parade.	
"	17		Bathing Parade - Route March.	
"	18		Cleaning billet.	
"	19		Church Parade.	
"	20		Advanced party of 17th Div. cyclists with two officers arrived to take over. One officer + a dozen men went as an advanced party to Morris to take over the 17th Company's billets	
"	21		The Company proceeded to Morris by platoons, starting at 20 minute intervals from 7.15 a.m. Owing to some rain during the night, the road was very slippery + a large number of men fell out during the	

T2134. Wt. W708—776. 500000. 4/15. Sir J. C. & S.

Army Form C. 2118.

WAR DIARY
or
INTELLIGENCE SUMMARY.
(Erase heading not required.)

Instructions regarding War Diaries and Intelligence Summaries are contained in F. S. Regs., Part II. and the Staff Manual respectively. Title pages will be prepared in manuscript.

Place	Date 1916	Hour	Summary of Events and Information	Remarks and references to Appendices
Armentières	March		cont/	
Merris	21		first 1½ miles, all this being pavé (to Erquinghem). A lot of extra kit had been accumulated by both officers + men during the winter + this was reduced at Merris to normal amounts.	
Merris	22		Route ride to improve march discipline. Heavy rain + snow interrupted training.	
"	23		Inter-farm + platoon football matches during the afternoon.	
"	24		Cleaning of cycles + equipment etc. Kit inspection.	
"	25		Church parade at 9 am in one of the barns.	
"	26		Advanced guard scheme to Mt des Cats on parallel roads. Kit cleaning. Inter-farm football match.	
"	27		Inspection of Div. Mounted Troops by General Sir Herbert Plumer at 11 am. Company paraded in marching order + marched past with cycles. The General expressed regret that we were leaving the Army + remarked that the men were the smartest + cleanest he had seen for some time.	
"	28		Route rides by farms. Football match during pm.	
"	29			

Army Form C. 2118.

WAR DIARY
or
INTELLIGENCE SUMMARY

(Erase heading not required.)

Instructions regarding War Diaries and Intelligence Summaries are contained in F.S. Regs., Part II. and the Staff Manual respectively. Title pages will be prepared in manuscript.

Place	Date 1916	Hour	Summary of Events and Information	Remarks and references to Appendices
Meaux	Mard 30		Company proceeded by platoons to station at Godwaerselde at 10 minute intervals from 6 p.m. Entraining carried out with ease & despatch. 3 officers + 1 platoon having gone ahead to make arrangements. Train left at 11 p.m. + arrived at Longueau (3 miles E. of Amiens) at 10 a.m. on the 31st. One officer + 3 men sent on to Rebemont as advanced	
Rebemont	31		party to arrange billets etc. Company following shortly after. Owing partly to sudden change in the weather, hilly country + the cycles being heavily loaded up, a number of men fell out; these were marked down for special training later. Emplanes arrived about 7 p.m. Rest of the day spent in allotting billets, drawing straw, rations etc.	

21st Divisional Troops

Became XV Corps Cyclists 10.5.16

21st DIVISIONAL CYCLIST COMPANY ::: APRIL 1916 .

WAR DIARY
INTELLIGENCE SUMMARY

Army Form C. 2118.

21st Div: Cyclist [Coy?]

Place	Date	Hour	Summary of Events and Information	Remarks and references to Appendices
[Béthune?]	April 1st		Received Guard duties by 3 sections & 3 sections of section [?] with full kit. Men picked out as unsuitable for [?] going out for special instruction.	
	2		Church Parade at 10 a.m. keeping one Sgt to [?] Redheads & one P.O. visiting unknown	
	3		3 Officers sent to [?]-sur-[?] on billeting reconnaissance. Company practised advanced guard and by section keeping. Have stayed 7th Division Happy scheme during P.O. Company practised advanced guard scheme & reconnaissance on Tally Ho &c. - Lectures for N.C.O.'s during the afternoon. 9 N.C.O.'s sent to review the trenches to get to know the ground.	
	4		Company team played 21st Div Supply column during 1-1. Advance Guard scheme & reconnaissance on [Béthune?]. One Platoon fighting war game action. Reports & letter following during p.m.	
	5			
	6		Platoon training & shoot Route March & rifle exercises during afternoon	

WAR DIARY
or
INTELLIGENCE SUMMARY

Date	Hour	Summary of Events and Information
March 19		Report front of platoons & enemy & any experience ever week.
20		Working party went to work on For S&R dugouts in the dept & relief of no N&Cs men.
20		
21		Emp. to manage & teams & strong of anything unusual on Sgt. to 1 N.C.O + 21 men.
22		Officers at work recovering. No enemy signs.
23		Bench work at 9.5m. Initial total against selon bycheck as showered at 3 to for S.O. & men turned out. Working Parties of 21 men + N.C.O continuing.
24		
25		Remainder of Company furnish work during on L.H.G. train trenches.
26		Recce. Mener. Working Parties. Extended order drill - Working Parties. Working parties - Bullet thrown.
27		

Army Form C. 2118.

WAR DIARY
or
INTELLIGENCE SUMMARY.
(Erase heading not required.)

Instructions regarding War Diaries and Intelligence Summaries are contained in F. S. Regs., Part II. and the Staff Manual respectively. Title pages will be prepared in manuscript.

Place	Date	Hour	Summary of Events and Information	Remarks and references to Appendices
Bethune	April 28th		Working Parties Company paid to Schorck Trench.	
	29th			
	30			

30-4-16.

R.P.Boys. Major.
Commanding 31st Div Cyclists

T2136. W. W736—178. 500000. 4/15. Sr J. C. & S.

www.ingramcontent.com/pod-product-compliance
Lightning Source LLC
Chambersburg PA
CBHW081247170426
43191CB00037B/2071